ENGLAND

Designed and Produced by

Ted Smart & David Gibbon

WINDWARD

FROM the channel coast of Kent, where Julius Caesar landed in 55 BC, to the nuclear power station at Calder Hall in Cumbria, is a distance of some three hundred and fifty miles. Historically, the land it spans covers almost the whole story of the English people, and in the countryside there remains evidence of the passing of all those who created the English style of life through their laws, their architecture, their livelihoods and their pleasures.

On a clear day a direct flight between these two points reveals the cities, towns and villages, the farms and moorlands, roads, canals and railways that have played their part in the making of England and have given its different natural regions such rich and varied aspects.

At the start of the flight are the flat beaches of Kent that have tempted foreign invaders, from the Vikings, Anglo-Saxons and Romans to Hitler, but whose shores have foiled every attempt at invasion since William the Conqueror in 1066. To the west, at Dover, start the white cliffs, the beginning of the Downs, curving away to the west across the south-eastern counties and making a horse-shoe turn at the borders of Hampshire, in the southern counties, returning along the coast of Beachy Head and ending there in an abrupt and precipitous drop to the sea.

These chalk hills make south-eastern England a region of soft, rounded hills and wooded valleys in the center of which lies the Weald of Kent, a countryside of farms, orchards and hop fields filled with small villages of brick houses among which may be seen the tall, conical oast houses in which the hop was once dried to prepare it for the brewing of beer. In Kent, as almost everywhere in England, there are castles and forts, but along the coast are defenses somewhat different: martello towers, built to repel a possible Napoleonic invasion.

Canterbury, the first center of Christianity in England, lies in Kent and so do many abbeys and monasteries, some, such as Aylesford, near Maidstone are still used for their intended purpose, though many others are now country houses, hotels, business centers or just ruins.

Much of this area, because it is near London, is commuter territory linked to the capital by a complicated web of roads and railway lines. London itself lies in a great clay basin, a vast metropolis stretching as a continuous urban development from beyond South Croydon, site of England's first commercial airport, to north of the village of Harrow-on-the-Hill, home of the famous public school. In this vast area the living evidence of the past lives side by side with a fast-changing present.

As the close-packed buildings thin out, the view from an aircraft shows the countryside of the Chiltern Hills, a chalk ridge which stretches west through the home counties and dies away to the east into the flat lands of East Anglia, where the Vikings landed to rob and pillage, and where later the Dutch arrived to pass on their knowledge of canal building and land reclamation.

Beyond the Chiltern Hills the land flattens into the great Midland plain of England, a contrasting area of rich farmland and industrial no-man's-land. To the west lies the sprawling urbanization of Birmingham, Coventry and their satellite towns which link up through Stafford and its pottery towns with the Manchester conurbations, while to the east are the Leeds and Sheffield industrial areas of Yorkshire.

In the midst of the industrial turmoil lies the National Park of the Peak District, an outstandingly beautiful region of limestone rock where high peaks rise between steep gorges, and rivers run through labyrinthine caverns which provide an endless adventure and exploration territory for potholers.

The Midlands, once called the cockpit of England because they were the scene of continual strife between baron and baron, and baron and king, are also richly historical, with castles and great manor houses every few miles, wherever some natural advantage of topography could be exploited. Warwick Castle is here, as well as Nottingham Castle, Haddon Hall and Chatsworth, home of the Dukes of Devonshire, and an abundance of the great cathedrals and abbeys through which the Church maintained its control of its own government and land.

Beyond the Midlands lie the two counties of Lancashire and Yorkshire, and like a barrier between them the Pennine Hills that run from South Yorkshire to the Scottish border. To the west lies Liverpool, connected to Manchester by the ship canal and the port that, with Bristol, linked England to the New World. In this thickly populated area that stretches inland to Manchester and beyond to the Lancashire industrial towns, the industrial revolution of the nineteenth century took place and made England the richest and most powerful country in the world. Here were the iron and steel mills, the cotton industries, the builders of railways, ships, and giant iron constructions, and today they are still there, though many of them are diversifying into new kinds of technology.

To the east lie the Yorkshire towns, where heavy industry, wool and coal added their strength to industrial England. North of the industrial hubbub there is nature again, the natural wonderland of the English lakes that inspired Wordsworth and his friends. Alongside the northern Pennines the mountains of the lakes give an extra dimension to the English landscape, contributing to it the uncompromising beauty of their bare peaks and moors.

Only the southwest of England lies outside this imaginary journey from south to north and it is not inappropriate that this should be so, for west of Somerset is the legendary King Arthur's land, the last refuge of the Celts who defended it bitterly against the Anglo-Saxon invader, so that it has remained to this day a different land

---

Westminster Abbey left, founded by Edward the Confessor in the 11th century, is one of the most magnificent Gothic churches in London. Beneath its imposing arches all the coronations of English sovereigns since that of William the Conqueror in 1066 have been conducted.

with almost more affinity to Brittany in France than to the rest of England. This is a land of rugged coasts and bleak moorlands dotted with oases of vegetation. It is peopled, moreover, by a race which maintains a marked independence of spirit and has given England her most famous sailors.

The contrasting nature of the English peoples is a constant source of surprise, even to the English themselves, especially to those who inhabit the different regions of the north and south. To a man of Kent, and he must be born east of the Medway to claim the title (born west of the river he is a Kentish man), a man from Durham is as foreign as a Frenchman or a Scot. This is partly due to the various strains from which the English nation has been created: Iberians, Celts, Angles, Saxons and Normans were the invaders, but throughout history there have also been, and still are, immigrants, either seeking a better life or a refuge from persecution, who have added themselves to the community.

This cumulative racial integration has made a rich and varied race, resourceful, inventive, and despite their domestic disagreements, with a strong and determined will to keep their island identity.

But it is the differences that make a journey through England rewarding, offering to the observant eye variations in rural and urban backgrounds. The architecture for instance, ranges in materials through the timbered houses of the western Midlands and southern counties to the gray limestone cottages of the Cotswolds and Cornwall and the brick houses of the eastern Midlands, and in historical styles from classical Greek to nineteenth century Italianate, with many other influences in between.

Later, this tendency to imitate ran wild when the new bourgeoisie, created by industrial wealth, turned to Gothic, Venetian, French and Swiss styles of architecture, thus bequeathing to the present day an entertaining open-air museum of replicas as well as some delightful follies.

Where food is concerned, modern methods of distribution have done much to eliminate regional menus though some authentic local dishes are still expertly prepared, and the local product is usually superior to its mass-produced imitation. English cheeses are still produced in their region of origin: Cheddar from Somerset, Stilton in Leicestershire (and not strangely enough, in the village of Stilton in Cambridgeshire), Wensleydale from Yorkshire, and Gloucester and Derby from the counties whose names they carry. The crusty Devonshire and Somerset cream, produced there and served with strawberries, is still a great attraction at tea time. In contrast there are the solid northern dishes which the traditional hospitality of this part of England serves in copious helpings: Lancashire hotpot served with oysters when the tradition is maintained, pease pudding and bacon, and the universally eaten roast beef and Yorkshire pudding.

Two currents are constantly at work in English life, one tending to want change and the other to preserve the status quo; out of this constant tug of war there arises compromise, a truly English trait shared by all the disparate parts of the nation.

The melting pot of all the different ingredients that make up England is London, for it is to London that everyone goes to look for a better life and to enjoy the fruits of the country's labors. Young men and women from provincial towns and villages arrive each year in their thousands, setting up a temporary home in rooming houses as they search to discover themselves in the city's multifarious life. In summer they are joined by millions of others, young and old, who have traveled across the world to see and experience for themselves the life and history of the English capital. Their ranks are swelled each day by the commuters and shoppers, some of them heading for the City which becomes empty of human life after office closing hours, and others for the West End, where entertainment keeps the streets full until the cinemas, theaters and public houses close.

To London, and its permanent residents, the arrival of visitors is a stimulant which irritates some but entertains the majority. The city is used to absorbing outsiders and turning them into residents, and those who arrived as outsiders end up forgetting their ancestry, and become Londoners, whether of French, German, Indian, Polish, Welsh, Scottish or any other extraction. The four-volume London telephone directory is proof of the mixed origins of the citizens of England's capital.

London, though not the geographical center, is the key to England. This is where the cultural center of the country has been since the time of the Romans, and until recently it was also England's main port. Ships of all sizes used to enter the Thames Estuary, from the North Sea and the Channel, headed for London, and the eastern part of the city was a maze of docks and quaysides; since the reduction of maritime traffic, owing to the great expansion in other forms of transport and the advent of container ships, the docks have closed down and are now being redeveloped as a residential area for overcrowded London. As one journeys up the Thames the Greenwich Observatory, the famous Maritime Museum built by Inigo Jones, and Wren's Royal Naval College come into view and so do the famous tea clipper *Cutty Sark* and Sir Francis Chichester's yacht *Gipsy Moth IV.* Then further up, at the highest point accessible to big ships, is Tower Bridge, a massive nineteenth century mock castle straddling the Thames. It appears to dwarf the Tower of London on the northern bank, the central keep of which – the White Tower – was built by William the Conqueror. William's Tower is surrounded by walls with strong points and smaller towers, all of them rich in history.

The Bloody Tower is, perhaps, the most sinister, for it was here that according to some, the 'Little Princes', Edward and Richard, were murdered in 1483. Sir Walter Raleigh spent thirteen years here, and the prisoners of the Tower read like a roll call of history. Anne Boleyn and Catherine Howard, wives of Henry VIII, were imprisoned and beheaded, so was Lady Jane Grey, the ten-days' queen, and the Earl of Essex, favorite of Queen Elizabeth, who was herself kept in the Tower when she was a princess. One of the last prisoners in the Tower was Rudolf Hess after his arrival in England during World War II. To the north of the Tower lies the City of London, which has its own government and was the original London that Pepys knew. The famous diarist would not recognize it today, for much of the city which was rebuilt after the Great Fire of 1666 was destroyed in World War II and by the city developers afterwards. It is now an area of high-rise buildings devoted to finance and commerce. Nevertheless, the City can still show a glorious array of Sir Christopher Wren's churches, in the crypts of some of which are even vestiges of the city of pre-Roman times.

The City also contains the famous halls of the old guilds, the chief of which is the Guildhall, the center of government of the City of London for over a thousand years. Also in the city are the two great markets which furnish London with meat (Smithfield) and fish (Billingsgate).

To the west of the City, on rising ground, lies England's greatest Renaissance church, St. Paul's Cathedral, built by Wren and in which he is buried. To keep him company he has the tombs of many famous English artists; Reynolds, Turner and Constable among them, and the two military heroes of the Napoleonic wars; Nelson and Wellington.

A short walk down Ludgate Hill brings one to Farringdon Street, under which the Fleet River, once marking the city limits, runs. Up the former western bank is Fleet Street, the center of the newspaper world, where giant trucks piled with rolls of newsprint block the side streets, and vans packed with the latest editions of the national papers scurry off to newsagents and railway stations in their efforts to deliver the latest news before it has become history.

At the bottom of Fleet Street is Temple Bar, marking the boundary between the City of London and the City of Westminster. Here, the Gothic pile of the Law Courts rises up, and among the pedestrians stroll bewigged judges and barristers on their way to a case or to lunch. Off the main street the atmosphere of pre-war London still prevails around Lincoln's Inn Fields to the north, and in the Temple between Fleet Street and the River Thames. Here, built around gardens and courtyards, are delightful eighteenth century houses where barristers and solicitors have plied their trade since the time of King Edward I, when they

took over the area from the Knights Templars, whose former occupation is recalled by the Temple Church, a round building based on the Holy Sepulcher in Jerusalem.

There are good views down the slope on which this legal enclave is built to the River Thames. Along its embankment, where the road runs from Westminster to the City, several historic ships are moored: the *Discovery* which took Captain Scott on his ill-fated trip to Antarctica, H.M.S. *Chrysanthemum* and *President* and the *Wellington,* the floating hall of the City Livery Company.

The new face of London, which is merging slowly with the old, can be admired from any of the bridges that cross the Thames along this stretch. On a fine day or at night it is still a sight worthy of Wordsworth, whose poem *On Westminster Bridge* was written nearly two hundred years ago when the banks of the Thames were still green with the gardens of lordly houses.

The 'West End' of London is in the City of Westminster, the largest of the London Boroughs, which includes such famous areas as Piccadilly, Oxford Street, Regent Street and Bond Street, as well as Knightsbridge, home of the famous Harrods store. Also in Westminster are the main theater and restaurant areas of London, the great hotels of Mayfair, and the great palaces – Buckingham Palace, St. James' Palace and the Palace of Westminster, home of the Houses of Parliament.

The City of Westminster, in fact, contains almost all the places that the majority of people all over the world associate with London and in its streets, avenues, squares and parks is a constant pageant of London life. The luxury trades such as fashion, films, perfumery, jewelry and advertising all flourish in this part of the metropolis, and those who work in them populate the streets, mingling with the shoppers. The Household Cavalry, often seen in full uniform riding to fulfil their duties at some important event, have their barracks in Hyde Park, a vast, open area green with trees and grass, in the midst of which lies the Serpentine Lake. Westminster also contains many of the great museums, including the British Museum with its imposing neoclassical façade, the Tate Gallery and the National Gallery which overlooks Trafalgar Square, where Nelson, in turn, looks down from his column on the millions of visitors who every year perform the ritual of feeding the pigeons. From Trafalgar Square one can look down Whitehall with its many historic buildings, including the Banqueting Hall where the misguided Charles I was beheaded, to Parliament and Big Ben, perhaps the most famous clock in the world.

In summer these places are filled with visitors and London's citizens, and the parks with which Westminster is blessed more than any other city, are full of crowds enjoying a momentary rest or an al fresco lunch away from the hustle and bustle of the city.

From its busy center by the river London stretches away north to the heights of Hampstead and Highgate, between which stretches a great park (Hampstead Heath), formerly the haunt of highwaymen but now a piece of countryside which Londoners can enjoy. To the south lie the heights of Dulwich, another fine residential area, and beyond them the chalk hills of the North Downs.

The Downs stretch in a roughly horseshoe shape from the tip of Kent towards the county of Hampshire, in the center of southern England, and then return along the south coast towards Eastbourne, a seaside resort near which they come to a precipitous and dramatic stop. Between the two arms of the Downs lies the Weald of Kent, a rich agricultural area, and a shore line of low-lying land that has been chosen by invaders over the centuries as the landing ground for their troops. The Romans arrived first in AD 43 and set up camp towns. They were followed by the Anglo-Saxons and Vikings, then the Normans, each of whom established strongpoints, many of which later became strongly fortified castles. The castle at Dover, started in the twelfth century, still dominates the harbor, which is the busiest of all the English Channel ports. Along the coast there are other castles such as Deal and Walmer, and a succession of martello towers, stone forts built to repel Napoleon. Inland, too, the castles abound; evidence that feudal lords prized this rich and lovely countryside which lies just across the Channel from France. Arundel Castle, to the west, is one of the finest of all and belongs to the Duke of Norfolk, Earl Marshal of England.

The south-east coast is also famous for its seaside resorts, which became popular in the nineteenth century when the English set the fashion for seabathing. Brighton was a favorite of the Prince Regent, later George IV, whose taste for the exotic led to the creation of the oriental splendor of the Brighton Pavilion. King George V favored Bognor Regis, but Queen Victoria preferred the Isle of Wight, across the Solent from Portsmouth.

But it was the common people, encouraged by nineteenth century railway builders, who really turned this corner of England into the pleasure ground that it is still today, inspiring the kind of seaside architecture – piers, pleasure palaces, winter gardens and bandstands – that became standard throughout the world.

At the western extremity of this 'garden of England' lies the city of Winchester, England's capital during Saxon and early Norman times, and at its eastern end is Canterbury, the religious center of England. The two were once joined by a Roman road via London and by paths that followed the North Downs; the 'Pilgrim's Way' of Chaucer's time.

The counties to the north of London also possess chalk hills which give a gentle drama to the landscape, with rolling slopes topped by beech-woods and quiet valleys away from the noise and bustle of main roads. The 'home counties' include Oxfordshire, Buckinghamshire and Berkshire, and the Chiltern Hills of the last two lead, in the north, to the low-lying land of the county of Oxford.

All three counties share the river Thames which is at its most entrancing in this area and inspired such famous classics as *The Wind in the Willows* and *Three Men in a Boat.* The river winds across a verdant countryside and between wooded hills, passing through delightful villages like Marlow and Goring and pouring tumultuously over weirs as it winds its way towards London and the sea. At Oxford it flows past the colleges of the University and Magdalen Tower, where at dawn on the First of May a choir sings to the assembled company of boats that arrive for the unforgettable occasion.

Oxford has been celebrated as the city of dreaming spires and many of its more than six hundred historic buildings are embellished with enough towers, spires and pinnacles to confirm its reputation. Though a university city, Oxford is also busy with other commercial activities, including automobile production, and the town center is always a scene of bustle and movement.

At the western extreme of the home counties are the streets of Windsor, dominated by the vast mass of the Royal castle that began its life as a hunting lodge for William the Conqueror and is today a favorite 'weekend' home for the Royal Family. The castle is surrounded by a Great Park covering nearly five thousand acres. Across the river from Windsor lies Eton and Eton College which was founded by Henry VI in 1440.

Great houses abound in the home counties. Among them is Hatfield House in Hertfordshire, built by Robert Cecil, 1st Earl of Salisbury, Queen Elizabeth's Minister of State. It was in the old Hatfield Palace, part of which still stands in the grounds of the House, that Elizabeth heard of her accession in 1558. Other interesting houses are owned by famous people who played a part in English history: Cliveden, which has a magnificent view over the Thames near Maidenhead, was once the property of the Duke of Buckingham, Minister to Charles I, and more recently of Lord Astor; Hughenden Manor, near High Wycombe, was the home of Benjamin Disraeli; Blenheim Palace, near Oxford, the seat of the Dukes of Marlborough and built by the first Duke, John Churchill; and Woburn Abbey, in Bedfordshire, which was given to the Russell family, now Dukes of Bedford, by Henry VIII.

To the east of the home counties lies a vast area of rich, flat farming land that stretches to the North Sea. These are the counties of East Anglia – Norfolk, Suffolk and Essex. Though lacking the drama of the more mountainous regions of England these counties have a charm of their own that has inspired painters and poets. The landscape is easily recognizable in the paintings of John Constable who was born in Flatford Mill. Here is the living model for those rich hedgerows, towering elms and leaning willows and for those brick farmhouses reflected in the shallow waters of a ford, which appear again and again in his paintings. Crome, Wilson and the painters of the Norwich School are others who found the landscape subjects they were looking for in the East Anglian fields and skies.

In the predominantly flat landscape the church spires play a dramatic part, rising like landmarks over the fields and fens: Norwich Cathedral, second only to Salisbury in size, was founded in Norman times; Ely's unmistakable silhouette dominates the country around it; Bury St. Edmunds, where the barons gathered to plan the strategy that led to the Magna Carta, stands like a fortress over Angel Hill.

Another feature of East Anglia is the windmills. Though many have disappeared, there are still some of the great ones preserved at Great Chishill, Cambridgeshire, on the River Yare and at Saxtead Green. East Anglia also has its share of big manor houses; Holkam Hall for instance, was owned by Thomas Coke, who introduced new farming methods that turned East Anglia from a wasteland into the rich countryside of today; and Sandringham, the Victorian estate particularly associated with Edward VII and where the Royal Family still spend much of their time running a commercially prosperous farming estate. And there are castles: Kimbolton, for instance, once the home of Catherine of Aragon, first wife of Henry VIII.

In southern East Anglia, through Suffolk into Essex, the continuation of the Chiltern Hills gives an undulating character to the landscape but further north there are two very flat areas which, until the Dutch came to teach the East Anglians how to make use of this land, were subject to flooding. One of these areas, The Fens, stretches from the bay known as The Wash south-west towards the university city of Cambridge. In contrast to its rival Oxford, Cambridge preserves the almost idyllic atmosphere of a market town through which the river Cam glides past colleges, sloping lawns dotted with flowers, and woods. From the river the architecture of Cambridge can be viewed without the interruption of traffic or the crowding of later buildings. Kings College Chapel, with its great window and twin towers, stands just across the lawns. The beautiful Renaissance style of Clare College, Queens' College, named after the wives of Henry IV and Edward IV, and Trinity Hall, are all along the river which, by St. John's College, passes under New Bridge, named the Bridge of Sighs because of its similarity to the famous bridge in Venice.

The other low-lying area of this part of England is around the popular seaside resort of Great Yarmouth. This is the Norfolk Broads. The Broads are a 200-mile maze of open stretches of water, lying inland from the sea, that provide ideal waterways for boating. As a result, the boat-

hire industry thrives here and so do the inns and pubs that line the waterways.

It was across this flat land and up these rivers that the Vikings came to pillage the inland towns of England and to demand ransom money. It was also in these fens that the resistance against the Norman conquerors was most fierce, with Hereward the Wake holding out longer than any other English chief. The exposure to a constant threat of invasion has tempered the spirit of the people of East Anglia and has raised from among them such stubborn fighters as Nelson and Oliver Cromwell.

The heartland of England lies across the center of the country in a great band of agricultural land, in which industrial areas blacken the landscape with slag heaps, derelict villages and smog-laden skies, but by no means obliterate it.

In the center of the great ring of industrial towns, which circle from Leicester in the south to Birmingham and Manchester in the north, eastwards to Huddersfield and then via Sheffield to Leicester again, there lies the Peak District National Park. In this unspoilt area of limestone crags and high rounded hills are some of the most beautiful valleys in England, carved by the rivers Wye, Derwent and Dove. The latter, flowing through a wooded gorge, has created one of the beauty spots of the area at Dovedale.

In contrast to the ring of big industrial towns that surround it, the urban areas of the Peak District are small and retain an old fashioned air. One of the larger towns is Buxton, a spa built by the Duke of Devonshire and whose architecture recalls that of Bath. Castleton, at the foot of the High Peak, is a village which boasts a Norman Castle and is the center of a network of underground caverns, some of which can be entered by boat. Near here at Noe is the beginning of the Pennine Way, a winding track leading north over the mountains to the Scottish border two hundred and fifty miles away.

To the south of the National Park lies the heart of England in more than a geographical sense, for on this undulating plain some of the historic battles in English medieval history were fought. Henry III's son defeated his unruly baron, Simon de Montfort, at Evesham in Worcestershire, Richard III fell to Henry Tudor at Bosworth Field in Leicestershire, and Cromwell's Ironsides won their final victory at Naseby in Northamptonshire.

The Birmingham industrial area sprawls across the south-west corner of the Midlands but as if to compensate for the squalor of the urban conurbations there is also some lovely countryside to the south around Stratford-upon-Avon and Henley-in-Arden.

Here, where Shakespeare lived, there were once thick forests which no doubt inspired his woodland scenes. Henley-in-Arden was in the midst of one, and its timbered houses were constructed of the wood which was so easily available. Nearby are; Warwick, with its great fourteenth century castle, the home of the powerful Earl whose political activities earned him the name of 'Kingmaker', and Kenilworth, once the home of the Earl of Leicester, favorite of Queen Elizabeth. Sir Walter Scott used the castle as the background for the novel named after it.

Near Kenilworth lies Coventry, a fourteenth-century cathedral city which gained modern fame for its destruction by the German Luftwaffe in 1940 and its rebirth as an architectural and artistic mixture of medieval and modern styles.

Eastwards towards Peterborough, and on the fringes of East Anglia, lies more history in the form of Rockingham Castle, built by William the Conqueror and used as a fortress for several centuries, and Fotheringhay, the place of execution of the unfortunate Mary Queen of Scots, who was imprisoned there for many years.

The most densely industrial part of England lies in an arc across the Peak District, between Liverpool and the Mersey River on the west coast and Grimsby, on the Humber, on the east.

Liverpool's heyday came in the nineteenth century, when steamships filled its docks and the Merseyside warehouses bulged with goods from the New World and Africa. Though much of its imperial glory has gone, the Mersey has acquired fame in more recent years as the home of the Beatles. Waterborne traffic still plies along the Mersey, however, and sails up the Manchester Ship Canal to the city, named Mancunium by the Romans who built it in the time of the Emperor Agricola. The canal enabled Manchester, the center of the woolen industry, to export its goods all over the world and it remains one of Britain's busiest waterways.

Much of the building in Manchester dates back to the nineteenth century when it enjoyed enormous prosperity as a manufacturing center and it increases in historic interest with every year that passes. The most imposing of all the edifices is the Town Hall, a vast Victorian masterpiece in the Gothic style reminiscent of the buildings of other woolen towns of the Middle Ages such as Bruges.

Manchester is more than a city devoted to commerce, however, and has a Fine Art gallery and its own orchestra; it also has its own famous recorder of the Mancunian scene in L. S. Lowry, the painter.

From Manchester in Lancashire to Leeds in Yorkshire is but a few miles. Once, during the Wars of the Roses, the two counties were mortal enemies but today the road travels through a succession of industrial towns among which the names of Halifax, Huddersfield and Wakefield stand out. But even in the midst of the 'dark satanic mills' of William Blake there is countryside that has given birth to some of the genius of English literature. The Brontë sisters lived at Haworth and the village, with its steep main street, still has some of the atmosphere of their time, even retaining the inn where their brother became a too frequent visitor. The ruins of the house on the moor, which inspired Emily Brontë's *Wuthering Heights,* also still exist.

To the south lie more industrial towns, including Sheffield, noted for its steel and cutlery, and Nottingham, once famous for its lace, whose castle was built by William the Conqueror. The real hero of Nottingham, however, is Robin Hood, whose exploits in Sherwood Forest have become a universal legend. At Lincoln there is a great cathedral which stands high above the plain on a limestone ridge; a superb example of medieval architecture in Britain and surrounded by the remnants of a charming old village.

To the east lie the Lincolnshire Wolds, a rolling landscape devoted largely to sheep farming and market gardening. The coast here has sand-dunes and long flat beaches which attract the summer holiday crowds.

The great counties of Lancashire and Yorkshire, which have played such an important part in English history, lie across the country to the north. They are both counties of contrast with their southern extremities plunged into the heart of industrial England and the north dominated by mountains and moorland. Yorkshire, together with Durham and Northumberland further north, were once the powerful Kingdom of Northumbria, and a stronghold of the culture preserved by the early church in the turbulent period between the Viking invasions and the arrival of William the Conqueror.

In the Pennine mountains, that run from southern Yorkshire to the Scottish border, are some of the most wildly romantic parts of the English countryside. Here there are bleak moors with wind-blown trees, little valleys through which torrents flow, tumbling waterfalls and the memorable Yorkshire Dales, where castles and ruined monasteries recall the drama of their past, when border wars and Viking invasions were a constant threat to a peaceful life. At Skipton, on the southern edge of the Yorkshire Dales, there is a castle, and nearby in an adjoining valley is Bolton Abbey. North of the Dales, Bowes and Middleham have castles, the latter once owned by Richard III.

To the north-east the rugged land continues to the Scottish border; its beauty and historical interest has re-awakened the interest of visitors to this area, and today in summer it is a favorite place for motorists and walkers. In Durham, a stunning city built on high land around a great curve in the River Wear, is England's most impressive medieval cathedral, and alongside it the castle that helped to protect the city from its enemies.

Between the mountains and the coast of north-east England lies the route to Scotland, passing through a gap between the Yorkshire Dales and the Moors that stretch to the sea at Whitby. It was from Whitby that Captain Cook sailed in his barque to Deptford and Plymouth, where he equipped his ship for his voyage of exploration to the Pacific. Also in Whitby is one of the earliest abbeys in England.

The route through the gap joins all the great cities of the north-east, Newcastle-upon-Tyne on Hadrian's Wall in the north, Durham, Darlington, birthplace of George Stephenson's Railway, and York. This Roman city was lived in by successive waves of invaders and today its attractions include the historic relics that remain within its walls which are medieval but built on Roman foundations. In the city are numerous churches dating from the twelfth century and culminating in the lovely Minster, the stained glass of which rivals that of any other cathedral in the world. Also in York is the Railway Museum, in which the whole story of the development of one of the world's greatest civilizing forces is preserved.

The north-western side of England, which includes the counties of Cheshire in the south, a green agricultural land, and Lancashire, culminates in Cumbria, one of the most poetic of all England's regions. The English Lakes, though small in area compared to some of the other lakeland areas of the world, have a variety that is unparaleled. Here there are long lakes with tree clad-slopes like Coniston and Windermere, wild, scree-enclosed stretches as on Wast water, the soft beauty of Buttermere, and somber little tarns found among the mountain summits.

It is not surprising that some of England's greatest poets and writers chose to live in the Lake District. Sir Hugh Walpole described the character of several generations of lakelanders in his *Herries Chronicle* and few people will be unaware that Wordsworth, Southey and Coleridge found their inspiration here. So, more recently, did Beatrix Potter, whose delightful children's books became a classic in her lifetime. Another well-known resident of the Lake District was John Ruskin, the art historian, whose house at Coniston is open to visitors.

The Severn river, which rises in Wales, flows into England in Shropshire, south of Cheshire, and through the city of Shrewsbury before starting its journey south to the Bristol Channel. This valley, almost on the borders of Wales, saw much fighting in medieval times, but later became the peaceful land of the manor houses and farms that give it its character today. Shrewsbury itself is a fine old town which, like Chester, has some of the finest timbered houses in England. The forests from which the wood originated have long disappeared, but here and there patches remain as at Clun Forest, a place made famous in the poems of A. E. Houseman, author of *The Shropshire Lad*. Wenlock Edge, a limestone ridge, was another of Houseman's favorite places and also inspired Edward Elgar's tone poem.

Crossing into the county of Gloucester, the Severn has the Cotswold Hills on its eastern bank. That the Romans came here too is attested by a Roman-built road that runs along the river, and by a town, Cirencester, which was the largest in England, after London, in Roman times. The town continued to be important in medieval times as the center of the wool industry and is today a popular center for visitors to the Cotswolds.

These hills, with their gray stone villages, and their network of valleys in which many streams, including the Thames river, have their source, arouse a special affection. Broadway, one of the most popular, is known far and wide and its sixteenth century inn is as much a scene of bustle and activity today as during its coaching days.

The orchards and fields of the Cotswolds disappear as the land falls towards the Severn estuary and Bristol, where industry and shipping remind us that this has been the great seaway to the Atlantic since the time of the Tudors. John Cabot set off from here to Newfoundland in 1497 and here was the Society of Merchant Venturers, whose enterprise started England on the way to becoming one of the greatest trading nations in the history of the world.

Bristol lies inland up the Avon river which flows through a great gorge crossed by I. K. Brunel's Clifton Suspension Bridge. In Bristol today lies another of the great nineteenth century engineer's creations, the *Great Britain*, the first screw-propelled, iron-hulled ship, which was towed from the Falkland Islands, where she had been wrecked, to be restored at her birthplace.

Inland from Bristol lies an area of historical and geological interest, the highlight of which is the city of Bath. Many of Bath's lovely Georgian houses were built in the local golden-colored stone, and they rise up the hill from the River Avon in splendid tiers, in which crescents and gardens evoke the atmosphere of the eighteenth century. Bath was well-known to the Romans because of its therapeutic springs and there still remain some fine Roman ruins and the famous bath to remind the visitor of their presence. But Bath really came into the English limelight in the eighteenth century as a spa. Here the aristocratic and well-to-do of England met under the observant eye of Beau Nash, the master of ceremonies, who laid down the rules of behavior; everyone drank the waters and tried to find suitable husbands and wives for their sons and daughters.

Bath is one of those rare towns that has managed to preserve its unity, with row upon row of houses, many of them built by John Wood, reflecting the impeccable taste of early Georgian architecture. The lovely Pulteney Bridge over the Avon river and its elegant buildings were the work of Robert Adam, whose civilized touch is visible in architectural features of so many of England's great eighteenth century houses. Add Bath Abbey, built in the fifteenth century in the Perpendicular style, with its surrounding streets with shops and tearooms, and you have all the atmosphere of a Jane Austen novel.

From the county of Gloucester to Sussex lies southern England, the England that most people think of when they talk of the parkland landscapes hemmed in by rich hedgerows and the gentle hills crowned by woods. As in Saxon times, the land is mostly farmland, except for the great chalk plains of Salisbury and the New Forest in the Hampshire Basin. Through Wiltshire, the largest of the three counties, where people carried on the trade of weavers until the Industrial Revolution set up its mills to the north, passes the road that the Romans built from London to Bath.

Long before the Romans the land was inhabited by prehistoric people, many of whose living sites have been excavated in this century. At Avebury, a circle of stones recalls that of Stonehenge which lies further east on Salisbury Plain. Stonehenge, built over four thousand years ago when sun-worshipping tribes inhabited England, was constructed of stones reaching 21 feet in height, some of which are said to have been transported from South Wales – a formidable feat. Every year the Most Ancient Order of Druids meets here to watch the sun rise on Midsummer's Day. A large part of Salisbury Plain is used by the British Army as a training ground, as the flat, undulating land is ideal for tank maneuvers.

South of the Plain are the river basins of the Hampshire Avon, the Stour and the Test, all flowing through valleys with rich vegetation and grassy meadows, and providing fishermen with some of the best water in England. In southern Wiltshire the Avon flows through Salisbury, where the marvelous cathedral is one of the wonders of England. Its unusually unified style is due to the fact that Bishop Poore, who had it built, managed to bring about its completion in the short span of 38 years. Apart from its cathedral and the Bishop's Palace, Salisbury still retains a medieval atmosphere in its old timbered houses and inns. To the north of Salisbury lie the foundations of the old Saxon and Roman town of Old Sarum which was abandoned when Bishop Poore made Salisbury the site of his palace and cathedral.

Dorset, to the southwest of Salisbury, is an extremely attractive county which is fortunately bypassed by the main tourist traffic as it heads for the west of England. Though small in size it has a very varied landscape, from rolling chalk hills in the west, where it shares a boundary with Devon, to central moorlands and scenery of a more rugged character to the east. At the western extremity of its coastline is Lyme Regis, a resort lying at the seaward end of a steep valley. It was a favorite of the writer Jane Austen and is also notable historically for the landing there, in 1688, of the Duke of Monmouth, illegitimate son of Charles II, who failed in his attempt to take the crown from James. At Lyme Regis and all along the Dorset coast the cliffs provide a happy hunting ground for collectors of fossils, for these are easily found among the slabs of broken limestone rock.

Dorchester is the main town in Dorset and is associated with Thomas Hardy whose Dorsetshire novels – Hardy called the area 'Wessex' – depict the local towns under disguised names, such as Casterbridge for Dorchester. Weymouth, a few miles to the south, is a port from which Channel Island ships sail and it was once an aristocratic resort. George III is reputed to have taken his first sea bathe here, to the accompaniment of a chamber orchestra playing 'God Save the King'.

At its eastern end Dorset's coast becomes a precipitous one backed by the Purbeck Hills, from which marble is quarried and on one of the summits of which stands Corfe Castle, a splendid ruin, of a fortress besieged by Cromwell during the Civil Wars.

To most people, southern England must surely conjure up the picture of Hampshire with its rolling hills, its once royal New Forest and its great port, Southampton, the gateway to England for all those who arrive by sea.

Its capital, Winchester, was once the capital of England during the reign of the Saxon and early Norman kings. King Alfred and William the Conqueror both ruled from here and Parliament often met at Winchester until the fifteenth century. Today, Winchester still has a great deal of interesting architecture even in its humblest streets, with many buildings dating back to the thirteenth century.

Though rural in appearance, Hampshire has always played an important part in English history, particularly in naval history, for the great naval base of Portsmouth lies in its southern coast at the head of a peninsula protecting a large harbor. With the additional protection of the Isle of Wight standing out to sea, the ships of the British Navy could shelter from the westerly storms and refit after their tours of duty to the far corners of the earth. Fittingly, Nelson's flagship the *Victory* is now moored at Portsmouth among the uncompromising gray shapes of present-day warships. Though badly damaged in World War II, Portsmouth retains a few old buildings that recall the great days of naval life; along the front some of the old sea wall remains and the tower in the High Street was there in the time of Henry VII, the founder of the English Navy. Though the use of aircraft has diminished the importance and size of naval forces, Portsmouth is still lively with the coming and going of ships of all kinds and all nations, and Navy Week still draws the crowds from far and wide.

To the west, between the rivers Test, which flows past the port of Southampton, where every liner of note once called, and the Avon, lies the New Forest. This area of woods and heaths was the king's hunting ground for centuries, and to poach one of the royal deer was punishable by death. It was in the New Forest that King William II, Rufus, was accidentally killed by Walter Tyrrell and a stone still marks the spot today.

The forest is one of the most peaceful places in England and is enjoyed by riders, hikers, campers and lovers of the open air. Its villages are carefully looked after and have a bewitching charm with their thatched-roof houses and their greens where cricket is played at weekends; and from its upland heath there are views all over the Hampshire basin.

At Lyndhurst the Verderers, who look after the Forest, meet several times a year and administer judgements on forest laws, some of which go back to the twelfth century. Ringwood is another delightful Forest village on the River Avon and at Rockbourne the foundations of a Roman villa show that the Romans, too, appreciated the beauty of the New Forest.

Though Portsmouth and Southampton no longer see the great Atlantic liners that were frequent visitors, they see more of a more popular form of maritime transport; the Channel ferries. These ply back and forth all year round between the mainland and the Isle of Wight, the Channel Islands and the coast of France.

The Isle of Wight is a small rural island whose world-wide fame rests on Cowes Week, when the world's yachtsmen gather for the biggest event of the amateur sailors' year. Cowes itself can also boast that Queen Victoria often stayed there, at Osborne House which Prince Albert designed, and that she enjoyed, or perhaps suffered, her first sea dip in the island's waters. There is still an air of seclusion about the island, though in summer the crowds gather at the popular east-coast resorts of Ventnor and Shanklin. Here, and in the other villages of the island, there is a wealth of Victorian architecture which is preserved by the local inhabitants.

At Carisbrooke, the old capital of the island, there is a castle on a hill from which there are splendid views all over the island, which is only 23 miles at its widest point. Charles I was imprisoned here. Today Newport, which lies inland on the River Medina, has become the most important town on the island and is its capital.

In the west of England the people have lived for centuries on activities concerned with the sea, and they were sailors, fishermen, smugglers and wreckers and even pirates. The seafaring atmosphere still survives, particularly on the coasts of Devon and Cornwall. Inland in Somerset and Devon, there are orchards and farms growing apples from which various kinds of cider are made, and where Devon cattle are reared, and there are wild moors whose craggy, rock-strewn landscape inspired some thrilling literature such as *Lorna Doone* and the *Hound of the Baskervilles.*

This region of England has a rich history that can be traced back even before the Phoenicians, who came from the warm Mediterranean for the sake of the tin and silver that is still mined in parts of Cornwall. The legendary King Arthur, possibly in reality a Celtic chieftain who resisted the Anglo-Saxons when they invaded Britain in the fifth century, came after the Phoenicians. Arthur and his court are said to have lived at what is now called Tintagel on the northern Cornish coast, but his kingdom stretched into Somerset. It was in Somerset, at Glastonbury, that, according to legend, the Holy Grail was hidden below the Chalice Spring on Glastonbury Tor, a conical hill once surrounded by water and marshland and very likely the site of the Isle of Avalon, where Arthur is said to have died. Today, the ruins of the once great Benedictine abbey at Glastonbury still dominate the quiet town.

Inland, the moors of Exmoor, Dartmoor and Bodmin have a dramatic quality, especially when the great clouds that have traveled across the Atlantic billow over them. On the moors, ponies, deer and other wild life abound, and little villages with stone-walled thatched cottages give a human touch to the wild scenery.

Much of the coast here has become accessible to walkers with the completion of the coastal path that winds around from Somerset to Land's End and back along the south coast to Dorset. On its northern stretch it passes craggy cliffs, such as those at Hartland Point, where the Atlantic swell crashes onto the rocky coast and at Newquay it skirts the great stretch of sand where in summer, surfers ride the waves.

The most westerly point of Cornwall is the most fascinating section of the coast. Small fishing villages nestle under huge cliffs and the seas break on rocky bays where Drake, Raleigh and Effingham and their little ships once took shelter from western gales. Artists have lived for many years at Mousehole and Newlyn where the shops are full of their work, while at St. Ives, a town that scrambles down a steep hill to the harbor below, is the world-famous pottery founded by Bernard Leach. On the south coast, on the way to Lizard Peninsula, is St. Michael's Mount, another part of King Arthur's kingdom, where a conical island is topped by a monastery.

Where Cornwall and Devon meet is the port of Plymouth. Though heavily bombed during World War II, because of its importance as a naval base, it still has some of the old streets that recall the time when it was a village, from which the Plymouth Fathers sailed to America in 1620 and from which Captain Cook began his voyage around the world in 1772. Today Plymouth is still the landing point for sailors who have succeeded in some great maritime feat, such as sailing single-handed round the world, as Sir Francis Chichester did in 1966-67.

This southern coast of the West Country, with its mild climate and sub-tropical vegetation, is known as the 'English Riviera' and several large resorts have developed along it. Torquay is the best known, a large town that has spread over the hills that surround the protected bay where

Napoleon spent his last days on the *Bellerophon* before sailing off to exile and death on St. Helena.

England has been many things to different people: 'a fortress built by nature' to Shakespeare's John of Gaunt; 'perfidious Albion' to the French during the Napoleonic wars, when Napoleon himself dismissed her people as a 'nation of shopkeepers'; 'the workshop of the world' to Disraeli; 'a land of sleepy rural tranquillity and beauty' to Rupert Brooke, and 'a paradise of women, a purgatory of men and a hell of horses' according to John Florio, an English lexicographer of the sixteenth century. The sheer variety of the country and its people invites such opinions, all of them holding a grain, if not more, of truth. Most English people, even those who find plenty to critize, would echo the poet Cowper when he said "England, with all thy faults, I love thee still", for despite its reticent, at times withdrawn character, England is a place that exerts a strong pull on the affections. On some it is the desolate places – the moors and mountains – that will leave an indelible impression, on others it will be the crowded cities with their endless and confusing bustle; many will remember a summer day somewhere in the country by a leafy stream or at a village cricket match, others will think of England as a vast and living museum where the past survives and lives alongside the present. In total all the individual impressions add up to England, an island of extraordinary historic wealth, a place with a touchingly beautiful countryside and ugly industrial areas, a complete place reflecting the unity of an island people whose destiny made them for a while the center of the world.

Not far from St. Just, the westernmost town in England, the rocky headland of Cape Cornwall right juts out into the sea. The actual furthest point west on the mainland of England is Land's End overleaf, the famous granite mass tumbling into the sea at the end of the Penwith Peninsula.

In the picturesque fishing hamlet of Codgwith, a fisherman proudly displays his catch below while fishing boats wait right before the gaily colored stone cottages of St. Ives. Washed by white-crested breakers, Godrevy Island Lighthouse overleaf stands sentinel in the Bay of St. Ives, and beyond Land's End above Longships Lighthouse left perches on a lonely Atlantic rock.

Cornwall is steeped in the vestiges of history and legend: the stone ramparts of a 13th-century castle remain at Launceston below; according to legend St. Michael's Mount above is part of the lost kingdom of Lyonesse, where once King Arthur's knights rode, and Tintagel Castle left stands on the site of what was one of his castles. Gwithian's Lighthouse appears on the horizon right beyond Gwithian Sands and on a Treen cliff overleaf, "logan" rock, weighing about 65 tons, "logs" or rocks, at the slightest touch.

Legend has it that the huge granite rocks
bottom left *near Newquay were stepping
stones of the giant Beduthan. Newquay itself
top left is one of the leading resorts in the
South-West. The picturesque harbor of
Mevagissey center left has also attracted
numerous visitors, among them many artists
and writers.*

Polperro *above and overleaf has, despite
intensive commercialization, retained in its
lime-washed houses and narrow streets all the
characteristic atmosphere of a Cornish fishing
village. St. Ives too,* above right and below
*was once a busy fishing village which sprang up
around a small chapel built by St. Ia in the 6th
century. Today most, if not all of the fishing, is
done by holiday-makers.*

Viewed from West Looe below right, *the
houses of East Looe cluster in tiers around its
ancient harbor.*

In a lush, narrow combe between steep cliffs, *Clovelly* on these pages and overleaf is one of the show-places of Devon. Cars are not permitted to enter the village and the white-washed cottages lining the steep main street are decked with flowers for most of the year.

The mile-long beach at Seaton above sweeps from high cliffs in the west to the mouth of the Axe in the east.

Torquay below, in its superb panoramic setting overlooking the Tor Bay, is the largest and most famous of the Devonshire seaside resorts and Dartmouth right has been an important harbor since the Roman era. Today Kingswear left is closely linked to it by ferries across the River Dart.

A stone on the quayside of Brixham harbor overleaf commemorates the landing of William of Orange on November 5, 1688 and serves as a reminder of the historical significance of this area.

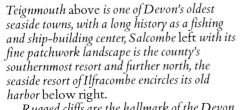

Teignmouth above is one of Devon's oldest
seaside towns, with a long history as a fishing
and ship-building center, Salcombe left with its
fine patchwork landscape is the county's
southernmost resort and further north, the
seaside resort of Ilfracombe encircles its old
harbor below right.

Rugged cliffs are the hallmark of the Devon
coastline below and it is understandable that
the craggy Valley of the Rocks above right
should have enchanted the poet Shelley. At
Sidmouth center right the cliffs are spanned
by the so-called Jacob's ladder which leads
down to the beach below.

In the village of Combe Martin overleaf
the local church carries one of Devon's tallest
towers.

41

Sidmouth above right, at the mouth of the River Sid, is a particularly attractive town with a pebble and shingle beach bordered by spectacular cliffs.

Widecombe-in-the-Moor above lies as its name suggests high up on Dartmoor. Its church which dates from c. 1500 has a high, pinnacled tower introduced by tin-miners keen to manifest their newly acquired wealth.

Thatched roofs are a characteristic part of the charm of Devonshire villages such as Buckland-in-the-Moor left, Bucks Mills below, Cockington right and Bickleigh overleaf.

Magnificent stained glass windows adorn the east end of the Chapel of Our Lady *left* in Exeter Cathedral – possibly the greatest glory of one of the most historic cities of Britain.

Bath in Somerset, which began in AD 44 as an important Roman settlement, is also a city of great historical interest. At its heart stands a magnificent abbey *above right* and *below* with, beside it, the elegant 18th-century Pump Room *overleaf.*

In memory of Edward Francis Black who died FFIF Pou... erected by his widow

An abbey these pages and overleaf *has presided over Bath since Saxon times but the original building was almost entirely rebuilt by Bishop Montagu in the 17th century and further 19th century restorations did much to influence its present form.*

The Roman settlement, Aquae Sulis grew up around the warm springs which made Bath the most celebrated of English spas and today the Great Roman Bath left *survives as an impressive monument to Roman Britain.*

Wells above and left, *in Somerset is particularly famous for its cathedral, begun in the 12th century. Its west front* below, *originally embellished with nearly 400 statues of saints, angels and prophets, is one of the finest in Britain.*

Only fragments remain of Glastonbury's 13th century abbey above left *and* right, *the last of a series on this site. Legend tells how Joseph of Arimathea came here to convert the English. As he leant on his staff to pray, it took root indicating that the saint should stay and found a religious house.*

The Devon and Somerset staghounds assemble for the hunt overleaf.

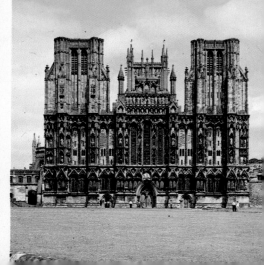

A graceful 19th-century spire rising 285 feet from the ground, rests on the fine 13th-century tower of St. Mary Redcliffe in Bristol below.

Bath was made a showpiece for 18th-century architecture, by architects such as John Wood the Younger who was responsible for the Royal Crescent right, an elegant open design of thirty houses in a sweeping semi-ellipse, and Robert Adam, who designed the Florentine, shop-lined Pulteney Bridge left and above.

A tribute to more recent design, the Severn Suspension Bridge overleaf, opened in 1966, carries traffic across the river estuary to Wales.

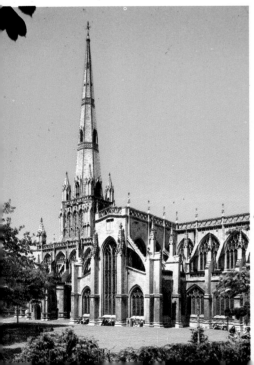

*At sunset the Severn Suspension Bridge below
casts an imposing silhouette against the
evening sky. The Clifton Suspension Bridge
left, above and above right, built by Brunel
in 1864, spans the River Avon at a point where
it flows between steep limestone cliffs. At
Cheddar Gorge right cliffs of this kind,
probably cut by a stream, now subterranean,
soar to about 450 feet.*

*Near Simonsbath the River Barle winds across
Exmoor overleaf.*

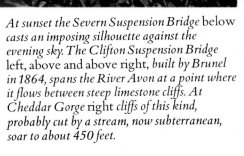

Among the many charming Cotswold villages with their characteristic stone houses, Upper Slaughter in Gloucestershire above right and overleaf is one of the most visited, but it was Bibury above that William Morris described as the most beautiful village in England. Apparently oblivious to time, the River Windrush still flows beside the main street of Bourton-on-the-Water left; old houses remain in Dursley right, and the ancient marketplace is still the focal point of Minchinhampton below.

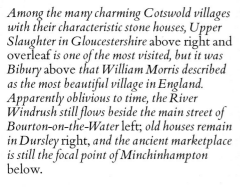

Tewkesbury, the site of a Yorkist victory in the Wars of the Roses, is now better known for its abbey *above and left,* topped by a fine 132 ft. high Norman tower.

Picturesque houses and unspoilt settings have made Gloucestershire villages such as Naunton *above right,* Buckland *below and Upper Slaughter* overleaf *the irresistible resort of those in search of old world tranquility and every effort is made to preserve the traditional. The lovely old manor house at Hidcote* right *is now the property of the National Trust.*

Peaceful country churchyards, water wheels and flowers are very much part of the appeal of the county of *Snowshill* above, *Lower Slaughter* below, *Dursley* above right *and Naunton* overleaf.

Chedworth right *is particularly noted for its flowers, among them countless lilies of the valley, said to have originally been planted by the Romans.*

In the middle of the Severn Valley lies the county town, the ancient city of *Gloucester* with its fine cathedral left *of Norman to early Perpendicular design.*

St. John's Lock at Lechlade left is one of the many tranquil corners of Gloucestershire and the River Swilgate which flows past Tewkesbury Abbey overleaf right is another such haunt. Chipping Camden's impressive church, center right with a 120 ft. tower, dates from that period. Despite its popularity, Broadway, in Worcestershire, above has managed to retain its characteristic charm. Overbury Church above right has an Early English chancel with a Norman nave and Pershore Abbey shown below and below right with St. Andrew's Church, dates back to the 13th century. Worcester Cathedral overleaf left is mainly of the Early-English to Perpendicular period.

Thatched cottages, such as that shown left or
Holland House in Cropthorne below right,
are typical of the county of Worcestershire
where the traditional art of thatching the old
black-and-white houses has by no means died
out. A rich historical heritage has been
preserved: Overbury Court above left, set in
beautiful gardens, is early 18th-century and
Evesham has retained the ruins of its ancient
abbey with its fine perpendicular bell tower
below and a half-timbered gateway on an
original Norman stone base center right.

The old water-mill above right completes the
setting of picturesque half-timbered houses at
Tewkesbury, while overleaf flower beds bring a
splash of color to the cottages of Broadway.

At a height of 1,024 feet, an 18th-century tower *below* overlooks the village of Broadway from its vantage point on the top of Fish Hill. From here the rolling countryside of Worcestershire *left* is clearly visible.

Springtime brings daffodils to the old churchyard in Upton Bishop *above* and Autumn lends its own distinctive character to Symond's Yat and the River Wye near Coppets Hill *right*. Below Symond's Yat the river continues gently on its winding course *overleaf*.

Herefordshire incorporates another very
beautiful part of England, in which thatched
cottages above and below left and black-and-
white houses above right, frequently festooned
with flowers or covered with clematis as below
right, stand undisturbed in meticulously kept
gardens. The town of Ledbury has carefully
retained its lovely old buildings, and its cobbled
Church Lane above, which connects the
Market Place and the church, epitomizes
Tudor and Stuart streets. The gracious timber-
framed manor house in Lower Brockhampton
below dates back to about 1400.

On a bend in the Wye River overleaf, Ross-
on-Wye stands silhouetted against a cloud-
hung sky.

The great Renaissance house of Longleat was built in 1556 by Robert Smythson for Sir John Thynne. Described by Macauley as "perhaps the most magnificent house in England", it still has fine state rooms and art treasures, among them *the state dining room* left, *the grand staircase* above, *the salon* above right, *the drawing room* right *and the dress corridor* below.

The village of Castle Combe overleaf is one of the prettiest in Wiltshire.

Spectacular tributes to the works of man, the
Avebury Stone Circle above, set up by
Bronze Age peoples c. 1800 BC, rings the
village of Avebury. Stonehenge, completed
c. 1250 BC, lends an air of mystery to the
Salisbury Plain right, and cut into the
hillside near Weymouth left, the huge figure
of the Osmington man (also known as King
George III) rides his gigantic horse.

The spire of Salisbury Cathedral, at 404 ft.
the tallest in England, rises from the "water
meadows" of the Avon below, while mossy
white cliffs drop sharply away to the sea near
Lulworth overleaf.

Dorset, with its heathland and quaintly-named villages such as *Affpuddle* above, is Thomas Hardy country. He was born in 1840 in a neatly-thatched cottage in Bockhampton left, and Shaftesbury, with its steep, cobbled Gold Hill overleaf, features in his novels under its old name "Shaston".

At Cerne Abbey the 15th-century mullioned three-storeyed gatehouse below stands as a memorial to a former Benedictine abbey and Athelhampton boasts a lovely 15th-century manor house with lovely gardens right.

The village of Corfe Castle, with its
undulating roofs, capping gray-stone houses,
has a quaint character of its own but it is
dominated by the stark, spectacular fortress
above it *above, above and below right and
overleaf. The castle is a monument to centuries
of cruelty beginning with the murder, in
AD 978, of 18-year-old King Edward ("The
Martyr") by his stepmother Queen Aelfryth.
Less sinister in its associations, Cerne Abbas*
left *nestles amid rolling countryside and the
River Stour flows under a bridge at
Sturminster Newton* below.

109

Not far from Lulworth lies the sheltered Man o' War Bay below right and overleaf and a huge limestone arch known as Durdle Door, which juts out into the sea left and above right.

Sheltered by Ballad Down, the quiet Purbeck resort of Swanage center right offers ideal sandy beaches for sea bathing. It is also renowned for its curious cliffs and rock formations such as Old Harry Rocks above.

Further west along the Dorset coast a lighthouse below warns of potentially hazardous rocks at the renowned Portland Bill.

Viewed from Ballad Down, lush fields roll away to the town of Swanage *above right* and Bournemouth *top and center left* is another popular resort on the Dorset coast. A little further inland, just above the Frome marshes, Wareham *bottom left* has retained a number of lovely 18th-century houses, and thatched cottages, such as the Three Airs Cottage *above*, are far from uncommon in the surrounding countryside and heathland. The small market town of Wimborne Minster *below* makes an ideal center for touring some of the beauty spots of Dorset and is well stocked with welcoming cafés.

The well-known resort of Weymouth *right*, now a busy port for Channel Island ferries, seems far removed from the town which Thomas Hardy immortalized under the name of Budworth, and Boscombe *overleaf* has become a busy hive of holidaymakers.

To many people Hampshire on these pages is synonymous with the New Forest, 90,000 acres of woodland planted over 1,000 years ago to become the royal hunting preserve of William the Conqueror. Set in this magnificent tree-studded landscape, however, are countless charming cottages and Lyndhurst left, the administrative center of the New Forest, defies the main-road traffic with its lovely old buildings.

Rivers and waterways bring a particular charm to the English countryside. Past Christchurch Priory bottom and top right *flows the picturesque River Stour, and the River Test passes near Longstock* center right. Lymington above and left, *situated on the Lymington River where it flows into the Solent, is a popular yachting center, while heavier shipping in the Solent converges on Southampton* below, *a vital transatlantic port.*

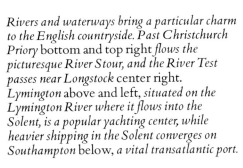

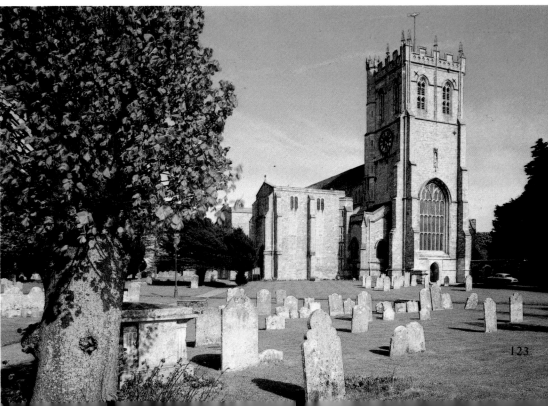

123

The estuaries of the Lymington and Beaulieu Rivers are polkadotted in summer with craft of all kinds, but above all with yachts destined for Lymington itself with its Quay Hill right and Nelson Place below, or for Bucklers Hard above left, a tiny village on the Beaulieu River, once a shipbuilding center which supplied forty of Nelson's ships for the Napoleonic war. Further up the Solent, Portsmouth above is a major arrival and departure point for the Isle of Wight ferries.

100 ft. cliffs circle the bay of Bournemouth with its superb sandy beaches left, and overleaf Yarmouth is a colorful and popular resort on the Isle of Wight.

125

Freshwater Bay *top left provides an idyllic spot for bathers on the Isle of Wight.*

On the Isle of Man, the picturesque tidal harbor town of Laxey is dominated above *by "Lady Isabella", the largest water wheel in the world. 72½ feet in diameter and capable of raising 250 gallons of water a minute more than 1,000 feet, the wheel was first set in motion in 1854.*

The Channel Islands are self-governing islands off the north-west coast of France, which belong to the British Crown and were originally part of the old Duchy of Normandy. In recent years many holidaymakers have been drawn to beaches such as Jersey's Portelet Beach shown with the Île au Guerdain right *and to scenes such as the floodlit Mont Orgueil Castle* bottom left *or the sunset at La Corbière, also on Jersey* above right. *Yet cliff scenery, like the imposing rocks of Creux Harbor on Sark* center left, *has remained unspoilt and the islands have retained such customs as the Battle of the Flowers on Jersey* below.

The waters off the English coast, made more challenging by the constantly changing weather and sea conditions, hold a particular fascination for boat-owners of all kinds. Summer brings power-boats and yachts, their spinnakers filled by gentle breezes, to these off-shore waters, where tall masted schooners still recall a great naval history.

The coastline west of Eastbourne is dominated by chalk cliffs rising to 600 feet above sea level at Beachy Head overleaf. At their feet stands the Beachy Head lighthouse, washed by the unpredictable waters of the English Channel.

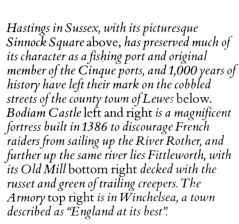

Hastings in Sussex, with its picturesque
Sinnock Square above, has preserved much of
its character as a fishing port and original
member of the Cinque ports, and 1,000 years of
history have left their mark on the cobbled
streets of the county town of *Lewes* below.
Bodiam Castle left and right *is a magnificent
fortress built in 1386 to discourage French
raiders from sailing up the River Rother, and
further up the same river lies Fittleworth, with
its *Old Mill* bottom right *decked with the
russet and green of trailing creepers. The
Armory* top right *is in Winchelsea, a town
described as "England at its best".*

It was at Bosham overleaf *that King Canute
is said to have commanded the tide to roll back.*

The Normans built the original Arundel Castle to defend the valley of the Arun River against raiders and its successor still dominates the valley above. In the water meadows of the Arun also, lie the clustered houses of Burpham left, typical of many West Sussex villages such as Thakeham below or Midhurst above right. Glyndebourne right is renowned for its music and opera festivals, instituted in 1934 by John Christy, who opened his ancestral home for performances by world-famous singers and conductors.

An onion-shaped dome and minarets adorn the Royal Pavilion, the Prince Regent's fantastic creation at Brighton overleaf.

139

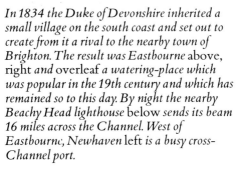

In 1834 the Duke of Devonshire inherited a small village on the south coast and set out to create from it a rival to the nearby town of Brighton. The result was Eastbourne above, right and overleaf a watering-place which was popular in the 19th century and which has remained so to this day. By night the nearby Beachy Head lighthouse below sends its beam 16 miles across the Channel. West of Eastbourne, Newhaven left is a busy cross-Channel port.

Shoreham-by-Sea above is a much-used harbor at the mouth of the River Adur, an idyllic haunt for small boat sailors.

Near Lewes the South Downs roll away in undulating countryside above right and on the downland turf above Wilmington appears the Long Man below. This tall figure, holding a staff in each of his outstretched hands, is believed to have been cut by the Saxons. Where the downs meet the sea between Beachy Head and the mouth of the Cuckmore River a dramatic cleft right has earned the name of Birling Gap. Water lilies left cover one of the five lakes at Sheffield Park Gardens, while overleaf winter brings snow and ice to a house near Wisborough Green.

Rye right and bottom left *was once a hill fort with formidable ramparts almost ringed by the sea. The sea receded in the late 16th century, but the town has never lost its character and individuality. The steep cobbled street* above, *leading to the old Mermaid Inn* top left *which opened in 1420, recalls the days when Rye was an important port.*

East Grinstead center left *has preserved its market town atmosphere and, in the heart of Brighton* below, *the Lanes are the surviving streets of the original fishing hamlet. Chilham in Kent* overleaf *is a picturesque village with a magnificent square surrounded by timbered black-and-white Tudor houses.*

Kent is strewn with villages, where time seems almost to have passed unnoticed. Among the most attractive are Farningham with its weather-boarded mill *above*, Ightham *left*, Chartwell *below* and Headcorn *center right*. Only the keep of the Norman castle remains at Chilham *top right* but nearby is a very fine 15th-century inn, and the Weavers in Canterbury *bottom right*, now a restaurant and gift shop is made up of a group of Tudor houses.

Lakey cottage *overleaf* overlooks a lake filled with water-lilies.

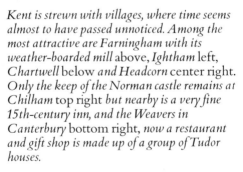

Kent is also rich in buildings of historical interest. Knole top left, one of the largest and most celebrated homes in England, dates from 1465 and served as palace for a succession of Archbishops of Canterbury. Hever Castle above is a moated 13th-century manor house in which Anne Boleyn spent her girlhood. Leeds Castle center left, a majestic fortress dating from 1120, was once the home of Catherine of Aragon and the prison of Elizabeth I before she became queen. The ruined Norman castle bottom left is the most important landmark of Tonbridge, and Scotney Castle right was originally a Tudor manor house. Most famous of all these buildings, Canterbury Cathedral overleaf, which dates from Norman times, is the Mother Church of Anglicans throughout the world.

Weatherboarded houses line the streets of
Tenterden below, *the birthplace of William
Caxton, the father of English printing, and
Tudor and Jacobean houses are the hallmark of
Chilham bottom right. The marketplace at
Faversham center right is surrounded by old
buildings, mostly dating from Tudor or Stuart
times, while beautiful half-timbered cottages
overlook the West Gate gardens in Canterbury
top right. In Royal Tunbridge Wells left and
above, the Pantiles, an 18th-century shopping
walk shaded by lime trees, has changed little
since the town was in its prime as an elegant
Regency spa.*

Ramsgate overleaf *is a major yachting center
but its harbor surroundings still resemble those
of a small fishing port.*

163

In the Napoleonic wars 3,000 French prisoners were kept in the medieval building right just outside Sissinghurst and today the beautiful gardens of this "chateau" are open to the public. At Cranbrook below, a splendid octagonal windmill, built in 1814 has been carefully restored and is still operative, and not far from Tonbridge left the traditional Kent oast houses, once used to dry the hops, have been converted into homes.

Aylesford above is a pretty village on the Medway, famous for its restored Carmelite friary.

Sunlight falls on the mist rolling through a valley near Dorking overleaf.

Surrey on these pages and overleaf *has miraculously succeeded in absorbing a dense commuter population for London, without sacrificing too much of its natural beauty. Wooded hills sweep across the northern part of the county and old cottages and villages remain unspoiled by their proximity to the capital. Even the towns have not lost their old-world features. The old wool town of Godalming* below *has narrow streets and buildings of Tudor and Stuart days.*

Modern developments have changed much of
the old River-Wey town of Guildford – Sir
Edward Maufe's new cathedral in simplified
Gothic now forms a conspicuous landmark on
Stag Hill above – but many interesting
buildings remain in the High Street where the
old Guildhall left bears a clock made and
donated by John Aylward in 1683 and the
Angel Hotel top right still possesses an old
wooden gallery and a coaching yard. In Quarry
Street there is even a keep below of a castle
built by Henry II.

The High Street in Dorking right follows the
route of the Roman Stone Street and boasts the
400-year-old White Horse Inn, where once
Charles Dickens stayed.

Wentworth Golf Club bottom right offers an
ideal course for golfers, while overleaf the
famous Derby is a gala occasion for sporting
enthusiasts of a different kind.

175

From Kew Bridge a footpath leads to the Thames north-bank area of Strand-on-the-Green where most of the houses are Georgian, and rising a 165 feet above the Royal Botanic Gardens at Kew, the Chinese pagoda below, designed by Sir William Chambers, has provoked much curiosity since 1761.

Traditionally the pond on the village green plays a vital role in English country life and the Surrey villages of Buckland below left and Chiddingfold right take great pride in maintaining theirs. Alford above left is renowned for its Norman church.

Winter transforms Outwood overleaf left and Smallfield overleaf right into a wonderland of frost.

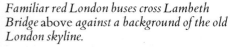

Familiar red London buses cross Lambeth Bridge above against a background of the old London skyline.

Epitomizing the new London is the futuristic silhouette of the Post Office Tower top left which houses, in addition to a great deal of technological hardware, a revolving restaurant.

Probably one of the most familiar views of London by night is Piccadilly Circus center left, with its famous neon signs.

A festive touch is added to Trafalgar Square and its beautiful fountains by the erection of an illuminated Christmas tree below left, an annual gift from the people of Norway, and to Regent Street below, by gaily colored decorations suspended far above the heads of Christmas shoppers.

The imposing clock tower of Big Ben stands as a symbol of London above the night-time traffic in Whitehall right.

Between Hyde Park and Green Park lies Hyde Park Corner overleaf on which stands Wellington Arch.

The crowned and blindfolded figure of Justice above *stands atop the most famous of London's Courts; the Old Bailey. Featured left are the impressive, and recently cleaned, Law Courts in Temple Bar. The smoke and grime of the years has also been removed from the stonework of the City of London Guildhall below left.*

Known simply as the Monument, the structure below *was built in 1672-7 to commemorate the Great Fire of London which started in 1666 and raged for five days, leaving two thirds of London devastated.*

The Lord Mayor of London's beautiful and elaborately decorated coach above right *dates from 1757 and, when not in use, may be seen in the Guildhall Museum.*

Pub lunches below right *are very much a feature of mid-day London.*

Hoardings and bright lights surround an unusually deserted Piccadilly Circus *overleaf.*

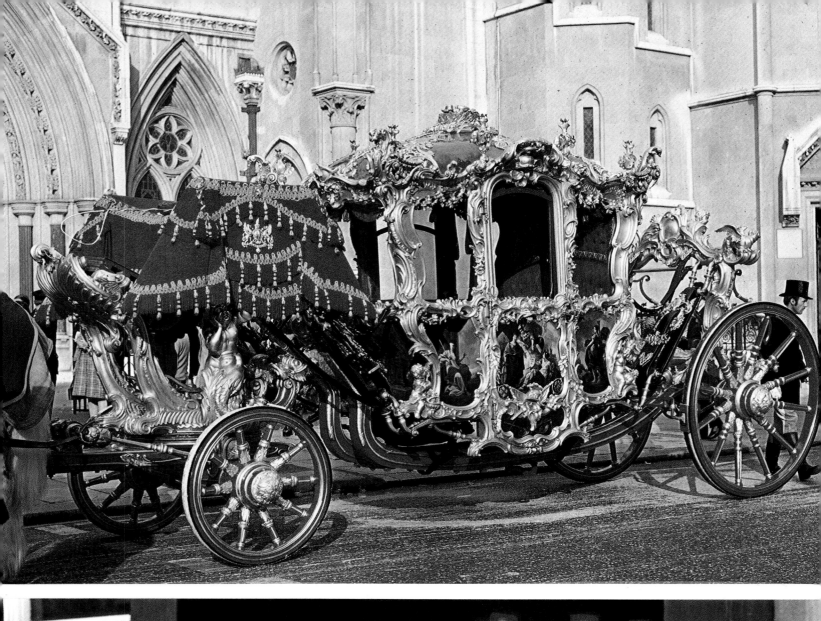

Wren's masterpiece, St. Paul's Cathedral, still excites the imagination. Designed to dominate the London of the 17th century, its sheer beauty and majesty still compare favorably with any of the more recent buildings built in the vicinity.

The 320 ft. Clock Tower of Big Ben presides over the Houses of Parliament and, beyond them, the River Thames overleaf.

191

London is far more than a collection of historic buildings, grand hotels, such as Claridge's left, or world renowned establishments like Sotheby's below.

The colorful Garter Ceremony overleaf, held at Windsor Castle, always attracts large crowds.

Windsor Castle in Berkshire these pages is a favorite home of the Royal Family and the largest castle in England, covering 13 acres. Founded by William the Conqueror, it first became a royal residence in the reign of Queen Victoria. The interior of the Curfew Tower the exterior of which is shown center left dates from the 13th century while St. George's Chapel overleaf is the finest example of Perpendicular architecture in England. The castle itself is still the scene of colorful processions such as that of the Garter ceremony top and bottom left, attended by Her Majesty the Queen, and Windsor is also the site each spring of the Royal Windsor Horse Show below.

Although inevitably dominated by its magnificent castle, the largely Victorian town of Windsor on these pages is itself very attractive and Church Street left, above left, above and right is one of its prettiest areas.

Royal Drive overleaf forms a suitably imposing approach to the largest inhabited castle in the world.

The Royal River Thames has a gentle and very English beauty as it passes towns and villages such as *Abingdon* below *and Molesey* left. It is also the historic river which borders the grounds of Hampton Court *above and right, the splendid palace begun in 1514 by Cardinal Wolsey and the favorite country home of Henry VIII. Five of the King's wives lived here and the ghosts of Jane Seymour and Catherine Howard are said to roam its corridors.*

The quiet scenes of English country life, the inspiration of so many artists and writers, have remained a reality in many parts of the country: far left *Boulters Lock in Maidenhead*, left *Marlow in Buckinghamshire*, above *the old mill of Hambledon*, above right *"Ye Old Bell" public house in Hurley* and right *Prior's Croft at Dorney, Berkshire*.

Blenheim Palace in Worcester overleaf is the grandiose masterpiece of Sir John Vanbrugh, built for John Churchill, the 1st Duke of Marlborough.

Established in 1214, the University of Oxford is the second oldest in Europe. The Collegiate system began in the late 13th century with the foundation of four colleges, among them University College above and Balliol below. Further colleges were gradually added, bringing to Oxford beautiful honey-colored buildings with "dreaming-towers". Christ Church left was founded by Cardinal Wolsey in 1525. Its college chapel, originally the Church of St. Frideswide is the cathedral of the diocese. The Perpendicular tower right is part of Magdalen College and, like the punts, very much part of Oxford tradition. Here at 5am on May Day the choristers sing.

Merton *bottom left and seen* overleaf *from Christchurch Meadows is one of the oldest colleges. It was founded by Walter de Merton, Bishop of Rochester in 1264 and the old city wall still encloses part of the college.* Oriel *top left was endowed by Edward II in 1326 but its earliest surviving buildings date from the 17th century.* Magdalen, *with its tower and cloisters above, dates from 1458 and is still one of the most beautiful colleges.*

Oxford's "Bridge of Sighs", under which the Sheldonian Theater can be seen left, is part of Hertford College and below, viewed from Merton Street, are the Examination Schools' grounds. It is here that students from all colleges sit the University examinations. A more recent acquisition, Nuffield college right was founded in 1937 exclusively for postgraduate studies.

The Sheldonian Theater *bottom left was
designed by Sir Christopher Wren in 1644 in
the style of a Roman theater and is now used
for university functions such as degree
ceremonies.*

The Bodleian Library *below, which dates
from 1480 and now holds over 2½ million
books, is one of the world's most important
libraries and the neighboring Radcliffe Camera*
top left, *designed by James Gibbs in 1737, is
one of the university reading rooms holding
600,000 books in its underground store.*

The quadrangles *left and above right are
those of Oriel College and St. Edmund Hall
and the façade right is part of St. John's
College, founded in 1555.*

Like cricket center right, *punting on the River Isis* top right *is a traditional summer recreation. The Romans called the Thames at Oxford the Isis. Exactly where the Thames becomes the Isis and vice versa is not clearly defined but the river flows through this great seat of learning as it flows through Whitchurch* left, *Goring Lock* below *and Wallingford Lock* bottom right. *At Henley* above *it makes another claim to fame. In 1839 the world's first river regatta was held here and the tradition still persists* overleaf.

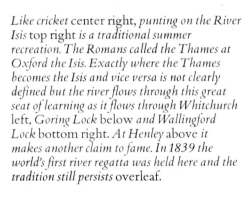

A Victorian-Edwardian seaside town with all the accompanying attractions, Clacton-on-Sea *left is also the site of a Butlin's holiday camp above. Leigh-on-Sea, another Essex resort below, offers quieter beaches and fine sea views, and further inland Finchingfield above right,* with its duckpond, green and church, is the epitome of the English village. The church set in a tranquil winter landscape *right is that of another such village – Stisted near Halstead.*

Suffolk villages such as Sapiston above and Cavendish center left have been the inspiration of many, but Suffolk is above all Constable country. John Constable was born in the county in 1776 and Willy Lott's Cottage in Flatford overleaf was one of his most celebrated subjects. The artist was at school in Lavenham right, the most resplendent of Suffolk wool towns with fine medieval timber houses. The market square is dominated by the Guildhall top left which at various times has been a prison, a workhouse and an almshouse, and the original Wool Hall has been incorporated in the Swan Hotel bottom left.

Kersey below is one of the prettiest villages. Here the street of dark-timbered houses runs through a watersplash where ducks still take precedence over cars.

Norfolk is perhaps best known for its Broads, or open expanses of water with navigable approach channels left and below. Together with rivers and man-made waterways they form about 200 miles for boating, and villages like Potter Heigham above are ever ready to provide for holiday-makers.

At Castle Acre above right are the ragged remains of the Cluniac priory, founded by William de Warenne, son-in-law of William the Conqueror, while Blickling Hall right, begun in 1616, was at one time owned by the Boleyn family.

31

Burghley House left, begun in 1552 by Sir
William Cecil, is one of England's greatest
Elizabethan houses, the home of the Exeter
and Cecil families for more than four centuries.
Despite the influx of holiday-makers, Norfolk
has preserved the best of its past. A ferry
provides a means of crossing the River Bure at
Horning below and a graceful windmill
presides over the quay at Cley-next-the-Sea
right. Lower Sheringham above, which
became a holiday resort at the end of the last
century, is still very much the old fishing village.

The pride of Cambridgeshire must surely be Cambridge, the famous university town on the River Cam. The university was established early in the 13th century and, as at Oxford, its development was marked by the foundation of colleges which stand nobly in a setting of river and gardens. Christ's College below left was founded in 1439 as "God's House" but was re-established under its present name in 1505. Trinity College above and overleaf, with its Nevile's Court above left, was founded initially in 1336 by Edward III then re-founded by Henry VIII in 1546. Clare College top right, originally University Hall, was founded in 1326 and Emmanuel bottom right was instituted in 1584. Among the other university buildings, the Senate House shown right with the Old Schools is an impressive adaptation of Wren's tradition to the Palladian style.

235

Queens' College top left *was founded no less than three times in the course of the 15th century, while Trinity Hall below was, remarkably, founded only once – in 1350 by the Bishop of Norwich. It is the only college still known as a Hall to distinguish it from Trinity College, of which the lovely bridge over the River Cam can be seen above. The "Bridge of Sighs"* right *links two of the buildings of* St. John's College *overleaf, founded by the mother of Henry VII, in 1511. Possibly the greatest glory of Cambridge, however, is* King's College Chapel bottom left, *considered by some to be the finest Gothic building in Europe.*

Yet Cambridge does not hold a monopoly on the county's fine architecture. Ely Cathedral center left, *begun in 1083, is a magnificent sight even from a distance.*

The lovingly-tended graves in the American Cemetery in Cambridgeshire on these pages are those of American servicemen who lost their lives in combat during the second world war. The view right shows the striking interior of the cemetery's Memorial.

THE MASTERY OF THE ATLANTIC
THE GREAT AIR ASSAULT

243

244

Castleton above is a large village, magnificently sited at the western entrance to the Hope Valley which sweeps down to Grindleford Bridge, and in the midst of the gentle pastoral Derbyshire scenery stands Chatsworth House above right. Built in 1707 for the 1st Duke of Devonshire, this is one of the great classical mansions of England.

Boats lie at their tranquil moorings at Whalley Bridge left, while the River Lathkill winds its way past Alport below to the tumbling waterfall right.

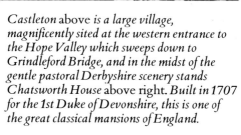

Despite the industrial development of the northern part of the country, Warwickshire still has its "leafy lanes" dotted with attractive villages like Barton on the Heath below and with imposing country homes. Packwood House above is a lovely example of a timber-framed Tudor building, begun in 1556 by William Fetherston. Its 17th-century garden of yew trees left is a symbolic representation of the Sermon on the Mount. Compton Wynyates right is another superb example of Tudor architecture and here too the stone and weathered brick are offset by yews and hedges tailored into neat, formal shapes.

Overlooked by the Church of the Holy Trinity, a statue in Coventry's Broadgate above commemorates Lady Godiva, who rode naked through the city in protest at her husband's oppression of the citizens.

North Warwickshire is dominated by Birmingham, a great industrial city, the center of which has been given over to such modern developments as the Bullring shopping center top left. It is Warwick, however, which is the county town on the banks of the River Avon. Here stands St. Mary's Church right with its 15th century Beauchamp Chapel and here also is the magnificent home of the Earls of Warwick, the finest medieval castle in England below. The superb photographs on this page and overleaf by courtesy of the Director of Warwick Castle Ltd are of the dungeon bottom left, the drawing room center left and the Great Hall overleaf.

One mile west of the center of Stratford-upon-Avon, the birthplace of William Shakespeare, is *Anne Hathaway's Cottage* on these pages. It was in this thatched and timbered house that Shakespeare's wife was born and here that he is thought to have courted his future bride.

Stratford itself on these pages *is a living tribute to the memory of Shakespeare. Overlooking the River Avon, the Royal Shakespeare Theatre* above left, below and right, *specialises in productions of his plays, and the beautiful parish church of Holy Trinity* above and left *is Shakespeare's burial place. His tomb and those of some of his family are marked by simple engraved stones in front of the altar.*

Downstream from Stratford, the Avon makes a broad loop round the picturesque village of Welford-on-Avon *above* and passes into Worcestershire, leaving behind it the quiet scenes of Warwickshire – the church at Lower Shuckburgh *below, the gracious tree walk at Kenilworth* right *and Wootton Hall* left, the lovely 17th-century house at Wootton Wawen.

Unique galleried shops have been preserved at ·the Cross in the very heart of Chester overleaf.

Chester, an ancient walled city on a sandstone spur north of the Dee, has preserved much of its medieval appearance in streets such as *Eastgate Street* above and below, lined with buildings, dating from the Middle Ages, and in its red sandstone cathedral right, which is mainly 14th century. Also in Cheshire, Little Moreton Hall left, a 16th-century moated manor house, is one of the finest pieces of black-and-white architecture in England.

Liverpool on these pages *is an important shipping, university and cathedral city and like the city, its "pubs" such as The Grapes* above and left *and the Philharmonic* below *have their own distinctive atmosphere. In the midst of the metropolis, Seeton Park* above right *provides a welcome retreat, while in its own quiet setting* right, *stands the Anglican Cathedral, begun in 1904, after the design of Sir Giles Gilbert Scott.*

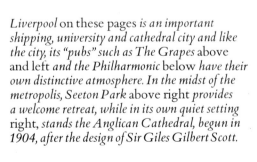

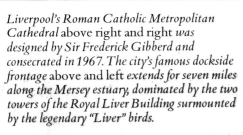

Liverpool's Roman Catholic Metropolitan
Cathedral above right and right *was
designed by Sir Frederick Gibberd and
consecrated in 1967. The city's famous dockside
frontage* above and left *extends for seven miles
along the Mersey estuary, dominated by the two
towers of the Royal Liver Building surmounted
by the legendary "Liver" birds.*

*The 15th-century Perpendicular Gothic
cathedral* below *is one of the showpieces of
Manchester.*

Blackpool on these pages is a lovely holiday town which began to develop as a recreational resort in the mid 18th century, and which has gained steadily in popularity ever since. The famous promenade runs beside golden sands for over six miles, dominated by the 518 ft. Blackpool Tower which contains the ballroom above. Every Autumn sees the illumination of spectacular decorations along the shore, and the pleasure beach on the South Shore, known as the "Golden Mile" left, is packed with funfair attractions.

The Lake District includes some of the wildest
and most majestic of England's countryside, yet
nestled beneath the bold austerity of the crags
are superb lakes like Derwentwater above and
overleaf and sweeping valleys dotted with
isolated farms below. Viewed from Kirkstone
Pass, at 1,489 feet the highest pass in the
region, Troutbeck Park and the Yoke Froswick
Fells left roll away into the distance, and
Kentmere right is dwarfed by some of
Westmorlands loveliest fells.

The landscape surrounding the central lakes has remained virtually unchanged since the days when William Wordsworth explored the hills and dales from his home at Grasmere *center right. The scenery near Tarn How* above, *Derwentwater* top right *and* Buttermere bottom right, *where the still waters of the Buttermere lake are hemmed in by high mountains, is timeless in its beauty. At* Great Langdale *below a narrow road picks its way through snow-capped mountains. The* Windermere suburb of Bowness *left offers magnificent views across the lake from its quaint, narrow streets, while* overleaf *Haweswater is still the most isolated of all the lakes.*

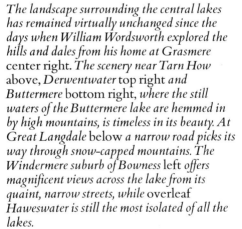

It was Grasmere's setting, below Helm Crag and Nab Scar and above Grasmere lake, which caused Wordsworth to pronounce the village above "the loveliest spot that man hath ever found", but the description could be applied to any number of beauty spots in Cumberland and Westmorland – Crummock Water above left, Elterwater left, Borrowdale below and the oval-shaped Derwentwater right.

Since time immemorial sheep have grazed on the Yorkshire moors and the wool trade has made Leeds, with its fine civic hall *below, the world center for ready-made clothing. York is famous for its old city walls* center right, *built on Roman foundations, which gird the ancient city for three miles. At Knaresborough* bottom right, *the River Nidd curls round the clustered town.*

The North Riding coast is punctuated with fishing ports and seaside towns such as Whitby left *dominated by the jagged sandstone ruins of the Abbey* above *and Scarborough* overleaf *crowned by the remains of a magnificent 12th-century castle. At Robin Hood's Bay* top right, *red-roofed cottages jostle for the sea front.*

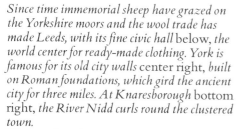

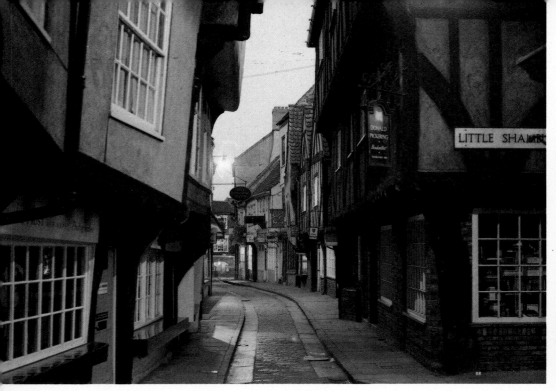

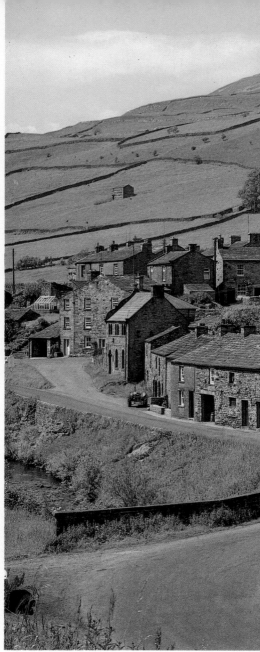

Inland Yorkshire is dominated by the Dales and windswept countryside like the surroundings of Malham *center left, protected by low stone walls and dotted with isolated farms* below *and villages such as Muker* above. *The River Bain* right *winds through Bainbridge across characteristic Yorkshire countryside. In York itself* top left, *old timber-framed houses lean towards each other across the narrow Shambles while, on the coast, the Harbor of Whitby* bottom left *is ringed by a fishing village of steep alleyways and hillside cottages.*

Yorkshire is rich in ecclesiastical architecture and York is second only to Norwich in the number of old churches included within its limits, among them the ruins of St. Mary's above. The city's splendid Minster left is of early-English to Perpendicular periods, and is famed for its west front and towers. The 12th-century Abbey at Bolton below was made famous by Landseer's famous painting "Bolton Abbey in Olden Times". Rievaulx Abbey below right was founded in 1131 and as such is one of the earliest Cistercian buildings in England and the quaint ruins of Whitby Abbey center right date from the 13th century.

Durham Cathedral above, *standing on a 70 ft. rock surrounded on three sides by the River Wear, was begun in 1093 by the Norman Bishop, William of Calais. Older still is the enormous stone pile of Bamburgh Castle* below, *once the seat of the first kings of Northumbria, and just off the Northumbrian coast, on Holy Island* right *stands the small 16th-century castle of Lindisfarne. The product of more recent engineering, the New Tyne Bridge* left *is one of the five bridges spanning the Tyne at Newcastle. Begun in c. AD 120, Hadrian's Wall* overleaf, *which runs for 73 miles across the width of northern England, is the most spectacular monument of Roman Britain.*